Bedtime Stories for Kids

Meditation Short Stories for Kids to Help With Falling Asleep, Learning Mindful Relaxation, and Calming the Mind. Dragon Fairy Tale Edition

Book 2

Table of Contents

Introduction

Thank you so much for your purchase of *Bedtime Meditation for Kids: Meditative Short Stories for Kids to Help With Falling Asleep, Learning Mindful Relaxation, and Calming the Mind. Dragon Fairy Tale Edition (Book 2)*. This book was written with the intention of helping your child with relaxation before bedtime. Controlled breathing and guided meditation can be the most effective way to ensure that your child is achieving their most restful sleep. In this stimulating world, it can be hard for children to wind down at night. This book is a tool that parents can use to ensure that their little one is calm and ready for bed.

Sleep meditation can be achieved through relaxing stories that are aimed at clearing the mind rather than exciting. These pages are full of guided meditations that allow for just that. Your child will also learn the fundamentals of breath control to relax their body and change their state of mind.

These stories are also meant to build vocabulary, inspire creativity, and reinforce the values that you are working so diligently to instill in your little ones. They will learn without ever realizing alongside a cast of loveable dragons and relatable children. What child doesn't love dragons? These stories are written about the topics that children are interested in, allowing them to venture to new worlds from the comfort of their bed.

This book offers the following benefits to parents:

- Relaxing tales that revolve around subjects that children find interesting.
- Stories that allow the child to enter into sleep meditation. There are also many helpful guided mediations within the stories.
- This book will help your child gain confidence and overcome their fears by allowing them to understand healthy emotional control.
- Bonding time allows parents to create memories that will last a lifetime.
- Help children find a natural way to restful sleep that does not involve expensive plans that don't work or medication. The tools used in this book will allow your little one to self-sooth any time they are stressed or overstimulated.

Chapter 1: Judging a Book by Its Scales

Sam was born in the town of Sonnet eight short years ago. To an earthly outsider, Sonnet would probably appear to be downright medieval. This realm had developed differently, though, due to the addition of one force: magic. Magic pumped through the very veins of Obligant, a planet that was otherwise very similar to our own during its feudal era.

The young man was the son of two explorers who had trekked their way through many of Obligant's most infamous wonders. His parents had solved riddles in the forest of trickster trees. They'd danced below the singing sky of symphonic rainclouds. The pair had been invited to the court of the most beloved king within their realm, and the three of them dined on confections and exotic candy until the sun came up. They swam alongside a herd of rare oceanic dragons on their winter migration path to the south.

Sam's parents told him all of these stories and many more. He wanted to be just like them; he wanted to see this magical world. The young man's parents were very protective of him, though. He was their only son and the light of their lives, so they were not so quick to allow him to roam around. Sam was still young yet, and he could do all of those things when he was older, his parents decided.

Sam was a free spirit with a lightning-quick wit. His brown hair and icy eyes mimicked his father's features. He was also thrilled by any opportunity to learn new things. He loved school and soaked in the lessons like a sponge. Sam was wise beyond his years and loved by everyone he has ever met. His personality just brought out the best in others.

It was a warm and sunny day when Sam and his best friend Michael decided that they were going to spend their hours gathering ingredients so that Sam's mother might reward them with a pie. There was a field to the side of the village that was riddled with berry bushes. The boys had the most fun picking berries, so they decided to go there first.

They dashed through the tall grass of the field, playing tag and rolling around in the way that young boys do. After some time, devoted to playing, the two young men began about the task of filling the pockets of their trousers with ripe berries. The smell that emanated from the area was sweet and soft. Sam could almost taste his mother's warm and buttery blueberry pie dissolving on his tongue. Michael must have had the same thought because the boys shared a smile before disappearing together in between the jagged branches of a cluster of tall bushes.

The pair were picking every berry in sight and trying to avoid the prickly nature of the limbs that seemed to incase them. As they plucked and pulled, the pair heard hushed voices. This was a popular pastime for the people of his village, so it was no surprise that they were not alone. The sounds were dainty and high pitched, so the boys knew that it must be a couple of younger girls from their area.

"Did you hear about the cave?" One voice asked, trying to whisper.

"What cave?" The other answered.

"Shhhh! I am not supposed to be talking about this. We must be quiet...The new cave in Crescent Cliffside. My father and the others think that it belongs to an evil bog monster like the last time." The first girl whispered again. A noise rang out from the field, and the young ladies stopped their conversation for a moment until they were sure they were alone again. Sam and Michael remained motionless and out of sight so that they could continue to eavesdrop.

"What do you mean last time?" The other girl asked.

"*Last time,* meaning twenty years ago. There was a cave in the same place, and the town's people stumbled upon it. It was a huge big monster that wished to pick people off from the village as they walked through the forest and near the cliff. It was gigantic scary looking." Girl one said.

"Wow, that is terrible. How did they get rid of it?!" Girl two said, not minding her volume again.

"Shhhhhh. They performed a raid on the cave at night. The grownups go to the cave with weapons and lanterns, and they scare the beast away!" Girl one said.

"What if it goes to another town to bother the people?" Girl two asked.

"Bog monsters belong in the bog, and hopefully that is where it went. Hopefully, that is where the beast goes again." Girl one said.

Sam and Michael looked at one another, knowingly. They were both intrigued by the story and determined to find out what the girls were talking about. The boys planned to continue gathering the pie ingredients. They would ask Sam's mom later that night.

The pie smelled like gooey heaven, and the boys were so taken with the scent that they almost forgot to ask about the monster. They remembered and excited stuttered through a recitation of the berry patch conversation. Sam's mother sighed and smiled at the boys.

"Boys... don't eavesdrop on others. It's rude to listen in when others believe that they are speaking in confidence. How would you like someone to listen in on your conversations?" Sam's mother asked.

"I realize that it was wrong, and we won't do it again, but please! Tell us about the bog monster!" Sam said, hoping that his mother would buy his remorse. She didn't, but the boys would never know that.

"Okay, so honestly, there was something in that cave all those years ago. That's as much truth as those statements possessed. The town's people had and still have no idea what built its home in that cliffside. You see, sometimes it's easy for people (even grownups) to allow their imaginations to run away with them. One of the residents came across the new cave on a hike and swore that they saw an ambiguous creature lurking inside it. The truth is, there is no evidence that a monster ever lived there. They left nothing sinister behind. The hiker was unable to give one solid detail about the creature.

The town's people allowed their imaginations to run wild. They were worried about their children and their families. I can understand why they were nervous, but there are better ways to go about meeting a cave dweller. Bog monsters aren't even real, as far as I or anyone else knows. It's just a catch-all term for *unidentified creatures*. I am embarrassed to tell you about this next part because it wasn't very kind or understanding of our little village...

Adults from the village waited until the cloak of night had fallen upon the land. They retrieved their weapons and their lanterns. The mob of scared town's folk were going to confront the monster. As the poor frightened creature noticed their lights approaching the cave, it fled.

The compassionate thing to do in that situation would have been to meet the thing in the cave. Speak to it and make sure that it wasn't ill-intentioned. Most cave-dwelling creatures are hermits who just wish to be left alone. NEVER make assumptions about others; it can be hurtful in ways that we don't understand until we are placed in that situation, ourselves". Sam's mother said thoughtfully. "I was only a child when this happened, but I wish I had stepped in or said something. I regret it so much."

"Then we have to do something! Maybe I can go warn the creature that they are coming so that it can go and hide!" Sam said enthusiastically.

"No, I am afraid I can't allow that. What if it is something dangerous? I can't let you take that risk. I will go and speak to some of the other town's people to make sure that they aren't going to do anything rash. Did the young girl say when they would perform the raid?" Sam's mother asked.

"No, I didn't hear that part. What if it is going to happen tonight? I can't just let them scare a poor innocent creature, mom." Sam said. Michael was quiet. He was not as eager to go meet an unidentified monster.

"Don't worry, honey. I will go and take care of it the moment your father comes home." His mother said, smiling. Sam hugged her and then grabbed his friend by the hand, claiming that it was time to go play once more before the sun went down. Michael said goodbye to Sam's mother and thanked her for the pie.

Gravel crunched beneath the boy's shoes as they traversed the road in the center of the village. They passed all the tiny wooden houses that sheltered the other residents. Every home was the same size and made of the most beautiful cherry tinted wood. Michael was inquiring about where they would go to play and what game they should indulge in. Sam stopped and looked at his friend with surprise, scribbled across his face.

"Michael, we are going to see the cave. I thought you understood my cues. We have to save the creature in the cave!"

"B-b-but... I thought your mom was going to take care of it!? She told us not to go. What if it's dangerous?" Michael said.

"My mom is going to *try* to take care of it. What if the town's people don't listen to her? What if she doesn't get to them in time? I can't let that poor creature suffer from the assumptions of the town's folk."

"I am actually pretty sure that you can. It is dangerous to go into the woods alone, Sam." Michael said.

"Well, good thing that I am not alone, then!" Sam said, lightly punching his friend on the arm.

Michael argued, but he was no match for Sam's willpower. Eventually, it was decided that the boys would go and check the cave out from afar to make sure it wasn't a monster before anyone went in. Michael was still nervous about the situation and did not like disobeying orders. He also couldn't leave his friend to do this alone.

The two boys slowly made their way to the edge of the woods. They would have to hike for a while before they reached the cave within the cliff. The sun was setting, but the boys were in a hurry, so they decided to carry on without light. The sky above them was a stunning pastel swirl of candy colors. Sam was always enthralled by sights such as this. He had a keen eye for beauty and was especially interested in the natural world and its color pallet.

Michael was less thrilled about the color of the sky above them and more concerned with their journey. He was a nervous boy and was not as impulsive as his counterpart. Thoughts of danger ran through his mind. His face began to coil in fear; his features weighed down by his own doubt. Sam noticed the look of worry on his friend's face. He stopped in his tracks and faced the boy, grabbing him by the shoulders.

"We are standing up for an innocent creature. We are doing the right thing. Maybe the wrong way, but we are doing the right thing. I can see that you are worried, but you have to be brave for the poor soul living in that cave." Sam said. Michael tried to smile to show that he wasn't bothered.

"Everything is fine. I am just worried about being caught in the woods at night." Michael said.

"We know this forest like the back of our hand. I think you are letting your fears run away with you. Let me help you." Said Sam.

"How?"

"My mom taught me to picture a balloon in your stomach. You breathe deeply to fill the balloon. Inhale slowly like me, count to four in your head as you breathe in. Hold that breath in your stomach while you count to four in your head again and then slowly exhale to the same count...one...two...three...four.

One...two...three...four. One...two...three...four." Sam Said. The boys stood there in the woods, breathing deeply. To Michael's surprise, this helped with his worry a little. His muscles also felt less tense, which allowed his mind to settle down some.

"Thanks, Sam. I don't want to be a chicken. I just get scared sometimes." Michael said after a few minutes of controlling his breath.

"You aren't a chicken. Fear is natural. There would be no such thing as bravery if fear didn't exist first." Sam said as the boys began to hike again.

The leaves crunched and slid beneath their feet. The young pair bravely stumbled along the trail as the sun began to sink below the horizon. It wasn't dark, but they knew that their light would soon be in short supply. The terrain began to slope and dive, which meant that they were getting close to their destination.

The pair spotted the cliff wall in the distance. Their hearts were racing. Michael wished that Sam had formulated more of a plan before they had set off on this so-called adventure. Sam was thinking with his heart rather than his head.

Sam and Michael made their way along the bottom of the ledge, looking for the cut-out mouth of the cave. They finally happened along a clearing with disturbed dirt. The branches of some of the nearby trees looked as though they had been torn down. They had found the entrance to the cave. The boys both grew silent as they stood and watched the dark mouth of the cave under fading light.

To their surprise, a small creature popped out. It was dark, but the boys could tell that it was no taller than themselves. The small being pranced to the center of the clearing and plopped down in the dirt. It was finally made visible by the fleeting light. It was then that Sam realized that they were looking at a small dragon. Dragons were so rare in their area, and Sam had never seen one in person.

Sam moved as though he were going to approach it, and Michael grabbed his arm to prevent him from going any further. The brave young man gently pulled his shoulder away from his friend; he had to warn the young dragon what was coming. He said hello, so that the creature might not be startled by the presence of someone else and began approaching.

The young dragon looked fearful, as though it might run away. To Sam's surprise, it never took a step to escape him. He slowly sat down beside the shimmering black creature and laid a hand upon it's shaking head. It was beautiful beyond what he had ever been told in stories.

The dragon was a shiny obsidian black, which meant that it originated from the lava flows. Its skin was made of various sized and randomly shaped black scales that glittered in the dimming light. There was a small trail of triangle spikes from the back of its flat head, to the tip of its tail. Its eyes were black with streaks of brilliant flame color flecks. It looked as though someone took a shovel and busted a hardening piece of lava, revealing the red-hot lake below the surface. The liquid heat in the young creature's eyes seemed to shift and swirl. Sam could tell immediately that the creature would take his breath away when seen by the light of day. He knew that he was only able to observe a fraction of its majesty.

This creature was already familiar with humans, which made sense because their village was so far away from any volcanos. The young creature looked at the boy with a thankful sort of longing in its eyes. The dragon was timid but also so in need of comfort. No one in the village had a dragon companion because they were just so far away from the creature's habitats.

A selfish part of Sam wanted immediately to bond with the creature; to take it home, keep it safe. He wanted that mysterious friendship that he had always heard about in the legends. He wanted to watch it grow into its full glory while he came of age right alongside it.

Dragons choosing their partners was not so simple, though. The creatures had a say in their own lives, and no one knows how they pick their companions. The old stories claim that dragons can judge almost instantly if a person fits with their own personality. They can read things like loyalty, kindness, humor, humility, and courage. It was clear to Sam that the young dragon had been stolen by someone bad, from its home. The poor thing must have then escaped and found the closest cave that it could in order to shelter itself.

Dragons also do not speak the human language. There is an ancient bond that holds them to humans, though. Sam had never tried to access this bond before, but he had heard tales of how it was done. He stroked the young creature's head, repeating soft affirmations so that it would feel safe.

Sam decided that he was going to attempt real communication with the adorable beast. He sat cross-legged in front of the dragon and closed his eyes. He left his hand upon the head of the creature. Sam then focused on his breath, clearing away all other thoughts. Michael was watching them in wonder from the brush.

The young man breathed in and out, only listening to his inhales and exhales. He took his time, letting all of the extra thoughts and feelings pass through him. Sam was so relaxed that he had almost fallen asleep when he finally felt the presence that he had been waiting for.

It wasn't words. It was a feeling. An immediate understanding. He understood that he had been right about the young dragon being stolen. He could feel the heat against his cheek and smell the sulfur from the creature's homeland. He was filled with an overwhelming sense of love for the creature's parents. The poor thing was sad and alone.

By controlling the emotions and thoughts that he experienced in that moment, he was able to speak back to the baby dragon. He showed it love and kindness, allowed it to grasp the empathy for its situation, that was welling up inside him. He also warned the creature that it was in danger. He could sense the distress in its thoughts.

Sam was so nervous at that moment, but he decided to ask. He wasn't sure that his heart could take rejection from a being that he already loved too much, even though they had only just met. He hesitated, but only for a moment. Sam asked the dragon if it would like to be his companion. The young boy assured that adorable dark spot in the dimly lit forest that he would always care for it. He would always protect it. It, he learned, was a He.

The dragon conveyed that it didn't have a human name yet and offered Sam the chance to help with that, before telling him that it would love nothing more than to be his companion forever. A happy tear rolled down the boy's eye. He knew exactly what to name his new companion; he knew it from the moment they met.

The boy conveyed to the young dragon that it must follow them out of the woods at that instant, to avoid the misguided "raid" from the villagers. The two of them snapped out of their bond and stood up. Sam called his bewildered from over from the trees to meet his new companion before they all could dart out of the woods.

"Michael, this is Fate. He is my new companion. He is far away from his home, and we are going to be his new family." Said Sam. Michael smiled at the cute and slightly frightening creature before him, giving him a touch on the head. The young dragon seemed to love affection. Fate missed the reassuring touch of his parents more than anything. Sam would one day take him home to visit his family again. For now, the three friends began their long walk back home in a forest lit only by the moon.

Chapter 2: Learning Hard Lessons

There was a village within the Realm of Obligant known as Rosemere. It was a quaint town that bordered an enchanted forest. The citizens of Rosemere had a healthy respect for the magic that sometimes seemed to claw at the borders of their town, but they were not a magical area. Rosemere sat firmly upon the edge of the mortal domain. The residents were more aware of the wonders of magic that lay just beyond the trees than other humans in more inland regions.

The sweetly soft voices of fairies could be heard floating from within the forest at night. The children of the town speculated about the mysteries that were held just out of their reach. Strange lights and colorful flying creatures stirred wonder within all of Rosemere's mortals. No one dared venture into this forbidden forest, for that would surely invite unknown influence upon their homes.

Life in Rosemere was lovely. To us, it would appear primitive. To its residents, it was perfect. They had everything they could possibly ask for. More than most regions in Obligant, Rosemere had running water and a very active community courtyard. Gardens allowed for entertainment for old and young inhabitants. Food was never in short supply, and everyone was very polite. Music and singing were very popular methods of entertainment for the citizens, and everyone seemed to have a fascination with sound. Especially the honied voices of the town's youth as they would gather every Friday night and sing in the courtyard.

Rosemere had put forth some very promising young people. Ambition and drive were known to bloom in the outlining town. Ellie was perhaps the most-watched and driven young lady. She was outspoken and ready to take on any challenge that presented itself to her. Her peers feared her willingness to trample others to meet her goals.

Ellie wasn't all bad. She was assertive and quick to take charge of situations that required a leader. She was intelligent and generally kind to others. Ellie was also young and had plenty of time to work out who she wanted to be. She was usually the most ambitious and determined young lady in whatever room she was in.

Ellie's parents were unsure that they were going to be able to have a girl. They had given birth to two strong boys, but her father especially wanted a daughter to protect and guide. The couple had become so thankful for their miracle baby, that they might have spoiled her just a little. Her parents were some of the wealthiest members of the village. They used their wealth to provide every available opportunity for their youngest child.

She was a lovely and popular young girl with curly flaxen hair that tumbled around her small frame in loose coils. Her doll-like features ensured that most of the adults in her life thought that she resembled an angel. Ellie's peers were privy to a slightly more sinister side of the young lady. She was entitled and willing to do anything to get what she wanted, even if that meant breaking the rules.

The village school met in a tiny building that sat directly next to the boundary of the forest. It allowed the students to use the woods for supervised study, a favorite of Ellie and the other children. She also enjoyed her walk along the dirt path to her lessons every day; she skipped along beneath a canopy of ancient trees.

Each morning, someone from the village would knock on the doors of the other houses in the early hours of dawn. These individuals were paid by the residents to act as an alarm clock. The adults would get breakfast ready and prepare to start their day at work. The children would wake an hour or so later and begin preparing for school. Ellie was the sort of girl who would always lay out her clothing the night before. Her house was not the norm in the village. Her family enjoyed a two-story brick residence with wooden floors. The young lady loved the sound of her shoes tapping against the floorboards.

Ellie was particularly excited to get to school on the day that the children would be learning about dragons. The young girl had always dreamed of flying high above the rest of her city on a dragon that she'd bonded with, all by herself. She had made up a secret plan to one day leave the village and go find her companion. Ellie was going to search high and low until she found a dragon that was willing to match with her. She was thirsty for knowledge on the subject.

The young lady kept a secret notebook pertaining to her dragon hunt. She would write down anything that she was able to find out. Hearing that companionship would be the subject at school today, Ellie was elated. She dug her dragon journal out from beneath her bed and brought her favorite glass dip pen to class.

Ellie buzzed past the other children on their way to school today. She would **need** to secure her seat at the front of the class for the day's lecture. The legends of dragon partnership and communication were the subjects that she had waited for her whole young life.

She sat, listening eagerly to her teacher to speak about all the lore surrounding dragons. Ellie had this issue where she would only hear what she wanted to hear. She wrote down and seemed to process that the dragons are allowed to have a say in their bond, but you will see that she never actually learned this. Or maybe she just thought that she could bypass a rule or two. Either way, we have already learned that the creature must choose you. It needs to be able to empathize with you, in order for the bond to stick.

Obligant was home to so many different types of dragons that there was no way to categorize them all. Ellie was going to have a difficult time deciding what she wanted in a partner. Maybe a sea dragon? They were the most breathtaking shade of azure, according to the professor. Their skin was also slick instead of scaly.

Perhaps she would think about a desert dragon, but the creatures just seemed too basic for her. She didn't want something intelligent and stoic; she wanted to be paired with a creature that matched her own perceived boldness. It was imperative that her companion both look and act the part.

That night when Ellie returned from school, she dreamed of dragons. Her companion was a pastel purple dragon with dainty scales that were each no larger than an acorn. Her dragon was a young girl, just like her. She and her companion both wore crowns of pink roses. She sat atop her dragon as the stunning creature flew them both high above the ground.

The pair raced and flipped through fluffy white clouds. The cold moisture on her face made the whole experience seem real. She wrapped her arms tightly around the dragon's neck as it flapped its mighty wings. The webbing was a creamy indigo tone. Ellie thought that it must be one of the most beautiful colors that she had ever seen. She knew immediately that she would name the dragon Lilac. The two would be best friends for all of time.

Until she awoke to the town knocker banging on the door in the morning. She normally didn't hear his noise, but today was different for some reason. Maybe it was because she knew that this was going to be another lesson on dragons, and she was ready to take more notes.

Elle was going to be a dragon expert by the time she was done accumulating knowledge on the subject from her many different places. She could not stop thinking about her dream. Maybe it was a sign that she was going to get everything that she had ever wanted. She had heard rumors around town that the council was going to begin allowing residents to have companions live with them inside the town walls. Ellie had assumed that this was coming because they had never bothered teaching about dragons in class before.

She reached the schoolhouse on that day, to see all of the other students buzzing about in excitement. Ellie asked one of the children why everyone was so excited, and she was told that they would be venturing out into the enchanted forest today to witness a dragon in the flesh. The young girl felt her heart stop at that moment.

This was going to be everything that she had ever wanted. She was going to get the chance to see some real dragons. What if the dragon from her dreams is out there too? What if she meets a companion while all the students are out on this walk? There were a million thoughts running through her head. She decided that she was going to ask her teacher if she could try to communicate with one of them.

Her teacher shot down her request, telling the young girl that she was not yet ready for communication. Ellie always felt a misplaced sense of entitlement to do the things that she wanted to do. This was not appreciated by the other students or her instructors. She may very well be able to communicate, but if she were to try, then everyone else would be owed a chance too.

The teacher rallied the students around him to go over the rules for the day. Everyone was to stay close to the group and in watching distance. Ellie was planning to sneak away, but she got the distinct impression that she was going to be watched closely during the outing. Everyone was buzzing with excitement; they were all ready to be exposed to the magic that their town had so long denied within its walls.

The students were led out of the class and onto a trail that twisted and turned its way to the heart of the woods. The students could be heard chattering and speculating about the magic that they might encounter. The teacher had to remind them that they would see nothing if they were making noise.

The woods were dense and beautiful. Light streamed through the leaves, creating beams that found their mark on the forest floor. Birds all around them were singing and flying from branch to branch in an effort to get a better view of the passing crowd. The fairies were sure to be around there somewhere, but they were timid creatures, and it was unlikely that they would rush to meet a crowd of students on the prowl.

Dragons liked rocky cliffs, mountains, and caves. The class was headed toward the largest cave system in the area. None of them had ever been allowed into the forest before, but they had all heard tales of the place. There was a small mountain with a mass of damp caves that were rumored to drip crystals instead of water. It was said that if you shout your name into the shrouded darkness of the cavern, a mystical voice will answer with the name of the person that you will marry. Ellie knew this was an old wives' tale but was going to try it anyway. You never know with magical places.

It took no time at all to come across the cave. The entrance was much smaller and less grand than Ellie was expecting from the rumors. The teacher could sense the class's confusion and told them to wait until they ventured inside before they passed judgment. The class brought many lanterns to ensure that they would be able to see in the relative darkness.

The children all grew silent as they began their trek into the mouth of the void. The lanterns let out a small yellow glow, not nearly enough for the children to fully appreciate their surroundings. Occasionally you would hear someone tripping over the rocky floor and then catching themselves. There was also a constant dripping sound coming from the walls and ceiling. Ellie was disappointed to find out that it was water rather than crystals.

The children began to get a better understanding of how massive their surroundings were as they progressed. The teacher seemed to know the way rather well, which astounded the students because there were so many complex tunnels. A few of the children were questioning why they had been allowed to explore such a dark and scary place.

Soon they ventured upon their target. There was a rather large deep green dragon that appeared to be laying on a nest in a small cavern. She seemed to notice the group approaching, but she was kind. She wasn't angry with the children at all. She was very receptive and open. The teacher explained that she was his companion, and that is how he knew her location. According to the teacher, she was sitting on her eggs.

Ellie's thoughts began to betray her as the teacher mentioned the eggs. What would happen if she were to steal one for herself? Would anyone notice one missing egg? If she raised the creature to be her companion, then she wouldn't have to worry about potential rejection. This means that maybe she could just raise the dragon to be her soulmate.

She began to scheme. She would return to the cave at nightfall when the mother was away, and she would steal just one egg for herself. The cave was bound to be much more frightening than it was during the daylight. Ellie would have to come up with a way to mark her trail in case she got lost inside.

When night fell, she snuck out of her parent's house by being very quiet and sneaking through the front door. The young girl took a lantern and a spool of thread with her on her journey. Walking through the forest when the world was cloaked in darkness was unnerving. She moved slowly and stealthily by the light of the moon. She used her navigation skills to locate the correct path.

Ellie knew that she was doing something wrong, but she wanted that dragon egg more than anything else, and she was willing to face the consequences for her actions. This young lady had a lot to learn about listening, respect and empathy for others. These were lessons that she was going to running head-on into.

The heist went relatively smooth. Ellie tied the yarn to a tree outside of the cave and used it to guide her back out once she had successfully located the egg. The cave was much more ominous at night. There was complete darkness, and she could hear things dripping.

She swiped the egg and then made her way out of the cave. She was very careful on her way out of the cave, not to bump into anything and jeopardize the baby. She buffered any clumsiness with her own arm. The afternoon before, she had built an incubator in her room that she would use to care for the fragile dragon egg until it was ready to hatch. She was going to care for this baby more than she had ever cared for anything.

Ellie returned to class the next day to find her teacher looking frantic. He would not discuss what was wrong at first. Ellie already knew. He told his class that he had trusted them with the location of the nest, and someone had taken an egg. He would search high and low until he was able to find out who was responsible. Those baby dragons need their mother when they hatch. They were not ready to become anyone's companions just yet.

The young girl felt a twinge of remorse for taking an egg that didn't belong to her and for violating the teacher's trust. She didn't think that the mother dragon would miss one egg, but she was wrong. Ellie walked around the rest of the day, thinking about what she had done. How much she had hurt those around her.

The next day the teacher announced that he had spoken to the council, and they were going to delay the approval of companions within the town walls until someone turns the egg in. That was too much pressure for Ellie, and she decided that she would return the egg that night. When she returned home from school that day, the egg had hatched.

The poor dragon looked so scared and alone. Ellie was in way over her head. She was terrified of being caught with the dragon and felt so much sympathy for the confused-looking baby. She thought that maybe she would try and communicate with the small dragon to reassure it that she would get it back to its mother. It was so small, maybe the size of a baseball. Its tiny head housed two large eyes that looked perpetually betrayed. She knew that the little one needed its mom. She was ashamed that she had ever thought stealing a baby was a sound idea. This was the moment that she came to the conclusion that she needed to make a change in who she was as a person. She wanted to grow up to be a good person.

Good people have compassion. Good people take accountability for their errors. Ellie sat upon the floor cross-legged and placed a hand on the baby's small head and cleared her mind. She pictured herself as a tree. She controlled her breathing, channeling it into deep inhaling and exhaling. You can follow along with her mediation at home:

1. Close your eyes and take five deep and slow breaths, holding them for counts of four. Breathe out slowly, listening only to the sound of the air going in and out of your lungs. If you have any thoughts that are trying to creep in, just let them fade away.

2. Take another three deep breaths. Hold each breath in your stomach while you count to four in your head. As you exhale, visualize that your body is a tree trunk, and your branches are stretching outwards.

3. Feel your roots as they stretch out into the warm and moist soil. It is similar to have your toes pressed into wet sand at the beach.

4. Keep breathing deeply.

5. Feel the sunlight on your leaves as you sway back and forth to a gentle breeze. You are nothing except a tree that is feeling the gentle tug of the wind.

6. Feel the moisture that you pull through your roots, traveling its way around your body. Think of the water as

it passes through your feet, then legs, then torso, then arms, then neck and then your head.

7. As you continue to breathe rhythmically, imagine that all your branches are beginning to come back to the tree trunk. Your leaves are beginning to meld with your body.

8. Visualize your roots slowly and methodically pulling themselves from the soil and curling up inside you. Your extremities are returning to your body, and your breath begins to get gradually lighter.

9. You are finally a person again, but you can still feel where your branches used to be.

This is the meditation that Ellie used to connect to the baby dragon. When her mind was clear, she felt all of its sadness and terror. She felt terrible. Ellie realized that she was acting for her own interests and not in a way that was good for the baby or its mother. Tears began to streak Ellie's face.

The young girl knew what she had to do. One way or another, she had to take responsibility for her mistakes and she had to get the baby back to its mother. There was no way around it. If she wanted to become a better person, then she was going to have to own up to her worst mistakes.

She approached her teacher the next day and told him what happened. She told him that she realized that what she did was unforgivable, but she wanted to make it right. Her teacher was angry with her for feeling like she was entitled to the mother's egg, but he also recognized that it took a lot of courage to confess to the mistake that she had made. He told her that if she brought the baby back to him immediately after class, that no one else had to know. Ellie signed with relief.

"But do not think that you are getting off that easy. You did an awful thing, and I need to be sure that you learned from it. You are so much better than this and you could have just ruined your future with this." The teacher said. He then told Ellie that she needed to write an essay on the importance of compassion and why it is important not to act on selfish impulses. She was also required to help with a companion event that the town's government was going to host as soon as they allowed companions into the area.

Ellie agreed and took her time on the essay. She poured her heart out onto that paper so that her teacher would know she was sincere. He was so relieved to know that she was on a better path. She was such an intelligent and ambitious girl but must learn to respect the feelings and wishes of others. This was especially true if she were ever to have a companion.

And she was. She met her companion two years later. It was a stunning dragon with skin the color of roses. Her dragon was her soulmate; the two were so similar in every way. She was thrilled to have finally met a companion who was as ambitious and driven as she was. She and her companion ended up being very successful together. Ellie began nurturing her compassion and it led her to become a nurse. The young woman and her dragon are living a fantastically happy life.

Chapter 3: The Value of Listening

Being born a dragon is easy; it just happens. Becoming capable of controlling your powers and learning to fly is a completely different story. You will have trials in your life that test the limits of what you believe you can achieve. There will be moments of doubt and mistakes that make you feel as though you aren't good enough. That's why practice, preparation, and planning can be so important. Remember that failing at your goals is natural, but learning to pick yourself back up when times get rough can be the difference between being average and being phenomenal. This is a lesson that our hero, Avery, had to learn the hard way.

Avery, the dragon, was born and raised in Balmy Valley. His homeland was absolutely stunning. Most dragons in Obligant lived in a desert habitat, spending their days basking in the heat atop dunes and large stones. Balmy Valley was one of the few outliers, in that it was paradise. The valley nursed a warm tropical forest with huge Jurassic trees with limbs like a spider's web.

The flowers in Balmy Forest could be heard singing their magical song from miles and miles away. The flora loved to harmonize, making up beautiful masterpieces that could only be heard once before fading into time. The woods were dense and wet, perfect for a reptile.

Tropical dragons were boldly colored and very unique. Their bodies were brilliant shades of neon, like the flowers, plants, and trees that they lived among. They also didn't grow quite as large as desert dragons, but they still towered over mortals as seven to ten feet tall. Should you find yourself standing in front of one of these splendid beasts, you might first notice the intense crests sitting upon their heads. Wild ornamental displays varied from dragon to dragon but were always magnificent. Tropical dragons were also much quicker than their drier counterparts. These dragons were impulsive and explosive. They were more human in nature and temperament, and not quite as wise and all-knowing as other dragons. These aptly named Dragons of Paradise were also possessed of skills and magical powers, their abilities were random and based upon their genetics.

Desert dragons were large lumbering creatures (at least fifteen feet tall) with skin and scales the color of clay or stone. They were earthy beasts that mortals chose for companionship when they preferred a partner who was large, stoic, silent, and loyal. These dragons seemed to be born with the secrets of the universe swirling behind their dark and pensive eyes. They were thoughtful and strong, the perfect choice in a partner for most knights. Some desert dragons were able to exhale heat upon command. Only volcano born dragons were given the gift of full fire.

These were not the only two types of dragons in Obligant, but they were the most common. Avery's father was a desert dragon, and his mother was tropical. When Avery was born, he looked exactly like his paradise formed peers. The young dragon's body was a vibrant and mossy shade of green that was accented on his stomach by a deep indigo. The pale and iridescent scales atop his head were embossed in a circular pattern, giving the appearance of a glittery crown. Avery had large and innocent eyes that mimicked the blue in the deepest parts of Obligant's oceans.

As his parent's match of desert and tropical has not been tested before, as far as any of the dragons knew, there was some worry that Avery may never develop an ability. This would make him less likely to find a human companion and limit his options for the future. Avery didn't worry too much about this until his peers began coming of age and discovering their powers.

The family lived in a cave that was carved out of the side of a sheer cliff. A waterfall covered the entrance so that the family might live in peace. Avery's father was a magnificent desert dragon who could almost pass for being tropical, himself. He was a powder blush/gray color, the shade of river clay. His scales often reminded Avery of a sky before a rainstorm. It was unusual for a desert dragon to have any blue at all, his father was lucky for this. His scales made him more attractive to humans.

There were many villagers who fought over companionship from Avery's father. He finally bonded with a young wizard who lived in a cave himself, quite a distance away. His father picked the wizard because he was a moral man and was also keen to allow the dragon to maintain his independence. Many dragons are not given all of the options that their family was afforded.

The new wizard was friendly, Avery had met him once or twice. He rarely called upon Avery's father, and the two were content to live separately. This was rare for dragons and humans, but it meant that Avery's family got to keep him at home. The young dragon was always so thankful for his father's smokey blue scales. Without his unique color, his family would be living a much different life.

Avery's father was determined to help him develop his breath. He wasn't showing signs of magical ability, so he should have been able to produce warmth. That was his father's logic. The two began practicing every evening when Avery was home from his lessons. Warmth could be such a valuable asset, especially to knights traveling in winter. Another reason that desert dragons were so popular.

The massive amount of time that Avery spent trying to develop his abilities became very frustrating to the young dragon. Sometimes it seemed like the more he wanted it, the less he was able to accomplish. He was focusing so hard, and nothing was happening. He and his father would try and try. Avery's father was not so easily discouraged. He supported his son's relentless practicing and wiped up the boy's bitter tears when he failed. Young dragons could have a very tough time learning to express their abilities because they required the taming of emotions. Feeling frustrated only added to the difficulty of finding the calmness that allowed for control.

Avery's father began to sense his son's frustration. He showed his son that he needed to find his own path to mental calmness, but nothing seemed to be working for the little dragon. He was growing wary of devoting so much time to a cause that didn't seem as though it could be helped.

His father had an idea. The older desert dragon who had taught him to express his warmth could probably mentor his son to help him learn about his own. The elder had been around for centuries and was able to call upon the wisdom from generations of both humans and dragons. He would set out to ask the elder dragon for his help.

Avery's father did not tell the young dragon where he was going. He didn't want to get his hopes up in case the elder was unable to help or just didn't care to be involved. His father set out on the long journey back to the desert where he grew up. It had been ages since he had been able to visit the land of the sun, and he was both nervous and excited to see all of his old family.

Life in Balmy Valley continued as normal while Avery's father was gone on his quest. Every day new dragons were learning about their abilities. Magic seemed to be passing the young dragon by. He was beginning to resign himself to the idea that he could only be a method of transportation to his future companion. His mother told him not to think that way. Companions hold so much more value than their magical ability. She hated seeing her son so sad.

Avery was practicing on his own. He didn't seem to understand that his frustration was just hindering him more. The more upset and strained he became, the more difficult it was to calm his mind. There were always a million things to think about and a million emotions to feel.

When the young dragon's father returned, he had with him another dragon. He was a rusty red color with deep brown eyes. This dragon appeared to be much older than anyone else that Avery had ever met. He was intrigued by the newness of the stranger. When the situation was explained to him, he was thrilled to have help with his situation.

The two got to work immediately. The elder's name was Axe, and he was several hundred years old. Avery felt honored just to be in his presence and was excited to explore the elder dragon's wisdom. His father was such a competent dragon, so learning from the same teacher was going to be a dream come true for Avery.

Axe was going to be staying with Avery's family, in their cave. The older dragon seemed to be taken by the scenery around him. He was familiar with a never-ending sea of sand. So much green must be a culture shock to him. Axe explored some of the dragon community in Balmy Valley, taking in all of its beauty.

He was a tricky dragon to try to understand because his facial expression never changed. He always appeared to be very stern and almost blank. In the coming weeks, Avery learned that he was this way because it gave him the most control over his abilities. Most desert dragons are only able to produce warmth with their breath, but this one was able to summon the wind. He could cause a storm should he so choose. This control was fascinating to Avery.

Axe taught the young dragon that being submissive to your emotions was a giant hindrance to conquering your mind. Avery had always been very reactive, which was preventing him from reaching the peace that he was going to need in order to unlock his own warmth. He wanted more than anything to achieve the stoicism that Axe possessed, but just maybe not in such an extreme way.

Axe taught the young dragon all about controlling your breath. Sometimes, when you feel an emotion, that emotion can cause a reaction in your body that strengthens the emotion in a negative way. Controlling the airflow in and out of your lungs can allow you to regain control of your body's reaction to stimuli. Axe instructed him to take a deep breath in through his nose and then hold it for a moment before exhaling through his mouth. Repeating this process (at least five times) can allow for a feeling of calmness to grab a foothold in your mind.

After many hours occurring over many days, Avery was able to control his reactiveness. He was not blocking out his emotions, but rather, allowing himself to take a step back to feel things without the thoughts controlling his body and mind. This was a huge revelation to the young dragon, who was slowly noticing a warm rising up from his belly when he concentrated enough on stillness.

Avery's father could not thank Axe enough for his help. He offered to pay him or allow him to come and go from the family's cave as he pleased. Axe was stoic and appreciative of the offer, as was his nature. He told the family that he had a hunch that his work was not done. Avery's parents were shocked by this sentiment. They were sure that Axe had done everything that he possibly could for their son.

Avery's parents told the elder that he was allowed to stay with them for as long as he wanted to. Axe accepted their offer and set about creating a plan for the young dragon. If he was going to coax out any hidden abilities, it was going to require some advanced levels of mental control.

Axe told the young dragon that they were going to create a meditative paradise within the young dragon's mind. This would be an imaginary place that Avery could visit whenever he needed to. He told Avery to think of paradise, whatever that meant for him.

Avery's escape was a beach. He had never been to the ocean, but he had heard so many stories that he was able to picture it vividly in his mind. The elder helped by adding sensations to the experience. When the young dragon closed his eyes, it felt as though he was already there.

He stood with his claws dug into the warm blonde sand. The sea breeze whipped against his cheek. Avery could smell the air. It was a scent he didn't recognize; earthy with a gentle bitter twang. The sound of the waves crashing against the shore in a repetitive way was the most peaceful thing that Avery had ever heard. He was in love with his new escape.

Avery imagined himself below the summer sun, basking in the light. He almost felt as though he were melting through the tiny grains. All his worries would systematically fall away from him.

He and Axe built this land together so that he might be able to completely clear his mind of other thoughts. The lessons took time, and learning to concentrate through the stillness was also a task required time and patience to master.

When Avery's buried powers were finally revealed, everyone was shocked. Avery, himself, was more surprised than anyone. It happened randomly one day. He had already released himself to the transience of his emotions. Axe and Avery were practicing just like they would do every single day. As Avery was concentrating, a giant boulder began to levitate into the air. This was the first that anyone had ever seen a telekinetic dragon. Even Axe stood with his mouth open wide.

His mother and father's genetics had made him stronger than either. He was the best part of desert dragons and tropical dragons. Avery was going to go down in the history books as having one of the most impressive powers to ever be expressed from a dragon.

Chapter 4: Knowing Everything

Maritown Dragonian School was an institution that all of the young people of Obligant competed for a place within. The classrooms had known some of the greatest minds of the time. The school was devoted to teaching the best of the best with dragon companions, all about dragon care and general education. It was assumed among all of the realms, that those who establish a bond with a creature outside of themselves are greater than average mortals. They are gifted with added intelligence, compassion, courage, and overall power. Dragon companions are the most common creature bonds, so they are also the most supported by society. Dragons are thought to add a great deal of value to any mortal's life.

Maritown was the most bustling city in the entire realm. There was so much life bursting forth from the city walls. The whole area was run under the banner of tolerance and solidarity. People from warring cities could come to Maritown with the expectation that they will treat one another with respect. These progressive and compassionate ideals were meant to mimic the nature of the dragons that the city fought so hard to promote.

All of these ideals meant that Maritown was far ahead of the rest of Obligant. It was developed and thriving. The community wrote poetry and enjoyed art from all over the world. Food in

Maritown is exciting, decadent, and plentiful. The government was the fairest and forgiving of any other. The citizens were allowed to live out their lives in the way that they saw fit, with little oversight. The most important rule was: *Cause No Harm.* Residents were expected to conduct themselves in a manner that was respectful to the people around them. Should someone become a nuisance, they would be banished from the city. This was a terrible fate for anyone who had ever lived in Maritown because it was a verifiable utopia. Only the most serious crimes were ever prosecuted in a court. The penial system was so small and almost unnecessary.

Not just anyone could enter this city. There were requirements. This may seem counterproductive to the freedom that the city offered, but if rules were not put in place, then the city would be flooded. You must have a bond or be in the process of creating a bond with a companion creature. There are also several screening tests that must be passed before entry is granted.

Once a resident is accepted into the city, they are allowed to build their lives there. Any children are expected to also form a bond with a creature when they are old enough. They also have the choice to leave the city, and if they choose to do so, they are given enough money to set them up in another town and they are granted visitor's access. Access may also be given to others on a short-term basis, especially to children who are touring the school.

Legacy children born to residents of Maritown are given the best life in all of Obligant. They are set on a path to success, and every opportunity is handed to them. These children are nurtured to become some of the most productive and heroic adults. These individuals grow up the most sought after by the smaller communities because they are molded into leaders and then given a chance to make their own decisions.

The downside to all of this freedom and opportunity is complacency. When you are raised in paradise, paradise is average to you. You begin to wonder if there is anything better out there for you. You aren't as grateful for the chances that you have received.

This was the case for a Maritown born boy named Fin. Fin was growing into a brilliant young man; his parents were at the top of their respective fields. His mother was a teacher of literature and a philosopher. His father was a medical man, a learned man of science. The boy had inherited their brains and been handed the best education available. It was not his fault that utopia was a fishbowl to him; he was born into it.

Fin stomped along gilded streets, complaining that there was not enough adventure in his life. He was lazy with his schoolwork because he was so intelligent that he could get by with very little effort, even in the Maritown schools. Fin was kind and thoughtful, but it was also very difficult for him to remain interested in anything for very long.

The students that come from cities outside of Maritown are eager to soak up the knowledge that they are being offered. These children work so hard for their place within the city and are some of the most thankful and humble mortals in all of the realm. Paradise was not so lost on them, and they would do anything to cling to it.

Fin watched them in class sometimes, with horror on his face. How are they able to be so interested in subjects like History? The young man could not wrap his brain around the other life that the outside students had been born into. They were born on farms so that their parents might have cheap labor. They were plucked from jobs that were labor-intensive. These children fought to perform over and over again for the chance to see the giant marble schools of Maritown.

Architecture in the city was amazing and grandiose. It spoke to the massive privilege that residents enjoyed. The streets were solid slabs of swirling marble that were polished monthly. The buildings were also marble, which made the whole area look regal and surreal. Sunset caused an ethereal neon reflection from the stone city. Visitors had described the glow as otherworldly. Close your eyes now and imagine a city that is radiating a sherbet or cotton candy toned light. Buildings were trimmed in various precious metals. Gold was a favorite among the shopkeepers.

Fin passed all this beauty every day. He had known it for as long as he had been alive, and it was all normal to him. New arrivals walked around with their mouths agape and their eyes wide open. Unicorns were regulars within the city walls, which was also a sight that was new to most outsiders. Unicorns were rare in Obligant, living only in remote regions. In Maritown, they strolled the shining streets alongside their mortal companions. Their iridescent horns were dazzling all the children of the city.

Fin loved to see all of this excitement around his hometown. He knew in his heart that he should be working more diligently to maintain his residence, but that was easier said than done. He needed to find motivation. Fin felt as though he could learn to harness his willpower through finding his passion. He was, of course, going to bond with a companion too. He had already decided that he was going to find a dragon, but he was unsure of which type he wanted to bond to.

There was a bonding event scheduled in a week's time; Fin was invited to attend for the first time in his life. Dragons and a few select other creatures from all over the world would be invited to meet in the city square for a chance to meet the children who were born to the city. This offered students a chance to meet and potentially bond with their new companion. Fin was so nervous about the chance to meet all of the new beings. He was slightly worried that they would see the laziness within himself that he was, so far, unable to remedy and the creatures would all reject him. He was also nervous about the connection process.

His school had had special weeklong lessons that were meant to teach the students methods of communicating with their companion creatures. Fin had done his best to listen but had found himself zoning out and not paying attention. He was concerned that he had missed a fundamental secret to connecting.

The night before the event, Fin lay awake in bed. His mind was racing with thoughts that he was unable to stop. Tomorrow could potentially be one of the most defining days of his life. What if he messed it up? What if he wasn't good enough. The young man tossed and turned under his thick wool blanket. He felt that he was too old to ask his mother for help, but he was also unwilling to get no sleep before such an important event.

Fin found himself knocking on his parent's bedroom door. Was standing in a long dark corridor, with his ear pressed to the wall of their room. He heard what he presumed to be his mother shuffling around in the dark, probably trying to locate her slippers. She appeared at the threshold, groggy and smiling gently.

"Fin, my darling, is everything okay?" She asked the troubled looking young man. Her voice was so soothing; she could have been a singer if ever she had wanted to.

"Yes mom, I just can't sleep. Is there any way that you can help me? I don't want to be too sleepy tomorrow to find a companion." He said. His voice was shaking. This meant so much to him. The young man was frustrated that he could not control himself or his body.

"Of course, I can. Don't look so distressed. Sleeplessness is normal. We can fix you right up. I can show you a trick that will knock you out so quickly." She said, closing her door behind her. She touched her son's shoulder to usher him back to his own room.

His mother told him to go ahead and lay down; she would be right there. He did as he was told, and she returned with a stuffed animal in her hands. It was a knitted dragon that looked exactly like her companion animal. Fin wondered how she found so much time to be so creative. She plopped down beside him on the bed and smoothed his hair from his face before sitting the crocheted dragon down on him. She placed it at the top of his stomach while he was lying flat on the bed.

"Watch the dragon rise and fall with your breath. As you inhale, count to three, hold it, and then slowly release your air. Keep an eye on the animal's movements. It will raise up as you inhale and dip down as you breathe out. I want no talking, only listening. Really listen to the sound of your breath as you watch the dragon rise and fall... rise and fall." She stroked the young man's forehead. "Come get me if you're still unable to sleep after a while."

Finn agreed and let his mother return to her bed. He found this a little silly but decided to give it a try. He took in deep breaths from his nose and then released them. He watched as the stuffed animal rose and then dropped again. The young man felt himself growing tired. All of those racing thoughts were being replaced by his simply watching and listening to the sounds of his own breath. This is something that you can also try with your most favorite stuffed animal. Fin didn't even realize that he was being ferried away to dreamland.

His dreams were turbulent and intense. Fin awoke with no memory of his sleep, only flashes of white and blue. His mother was standing beside his bed, shaking his arm. She had a look of horror in her eyes. Fin's heart immediately, his heart sank. That was not a good look.
"You told me two hours ago that you were about to leave! You have missed most of the event. I have sent your father with his companion to try and find a creature that would be willing to

meet you, but I believe that they are mostly gone. Son... you said you were getting ready?"

"I must have been talking in my sleep. I can't believe that I didn't wake up. Dad is going to be so disappointed. I am so disappointed." Fin said. Sorrow hung from his words.

The young man waited for his father to return. When he did, he was sternly lectured about his self-discipline. Fin was so disheartened by his shortcomings. He told his parents that maybe he wasn't meant to live within the city walls. Maybe he was meant to live on the outside, in a surrounding town.

His father refused to accept his son's defeated attitude. He also told the boy that he had arranged a meeting with a dragon who had also arrived too late to meet the students. It was a particularly difficult candidate and not the usual type. The creature was going to be allowed to live within the city walls because it was so unique. The dragon had refused all of the students who were left behind with no companion, so he didn't want his son to get his hopes up. Fin's father told him that he offered to house the dragon in the residence that the family had built behind their house for their companions. This was only temporary, but he had hoped that it would give Fin an edge.

"Let me warn you, son; there are a lot of people interested in bonding with this dragon. She is rare but she is also very picky.

She has turned down some of the most accomplished members of our city and is downright refusing to meet anyone else at the moment. She will be resting for a few days. I suggest that you study up on communication if you wish to have a chance." His father said.

Fin was terrified by all of this information. He felt like he was way out of his depth. He also wanted so badly to have a companion. He decided that he would try to study up on bonding, as his father had suggested. The young man retreated to his room to read books from his parent's library.

He was distracted by all of the dry text. He found himself unable to follow it. Fin spent hours trying to teach himself the concepts behind the connection. It required the human to clear their mind completely. He eventually surmised that it might be similar in nature to the breathing exercises that his mother had taught him the night before.

That night he stayed up late trying to understand the connection techniques. When it was finally time to fall asleep, Fin's thoughts were racing again. He decided that he would use the stuffed animal trick again because maybe that would do more to teach him how to clear his mind than all of the rambling text that he was trying to interpret.

He was breathing and watching the stuffed dragon rise and fall again. As his mind began to clear, Fin began to feel something weird. He felt as though he was not alone. It wasn't words that he heard or a voice that broke the silence; it was a sensation. He felt as though his heart were swelling with love and understanding. Suddenly he was being watched over. The boy felt safe and weirdly frigid.

Fin was so enveloped with this feeling of peace that he finally began to drift off to sleep. The next morning when he awoke, something told him to check the companion house. It was as if he were programmed to walk there. He walked right past his parents and into the dewy grass of the backyard.

His dragon was standing in front of the companion house, waiting for him. When he saw her, he felt an intense jolt to his heart. The moment was so charged that the young man ran to her and threw his arms around her neck. His parents watched from the door in horror, expecting the creature to deny his affection. Except she didn't. The icy white dragon placed her head against the boy's shoulder.

She was stunning. A pearlescent glow radiated from the creature. Her features were sharp and lean, like shards of ice. Her eyes were the lightest shade of blue. Like the sea dragons, she had a slick skin instead of scales. Her wings were long and gracefully shaped like an inverse bow. The connection that Fin felt to his new companion was deep and mature. It felt like knowing beyond a shadow of a doubt that you have met someone who understood you.

She had heard the name Stella once and loved it! Fin knew this without being told. He called her by her chosen name, and he watched her icy blue eyes light up in delight. Stella was also thrilled to have met a mortal that she connected with. Fin's father was so proud that he gave him lessons on connection. Fin was so excited that he processed every word.

Through Stella, Fin began to learn more and more about himself. They communicated constantly; she showed him that she picked him because she felt that they were the same. Stella had also had issues with being bored and feeling like she had no self-control. She was one of the rarest dragons on the planet, being born at the polar ice caps. She and her small community reared their young in the same way that the mortals did, for the most part. She thought that she would never learn to fly; she simply could not pay attention during the lessons. She was always looked upon as lazy by the rest of her family.

Stella broke away from her family and taught herself how to fly. She learned that she just didn't process information like everyone else. The stunning white dragon had to try things for herself. Being told or explained to did very little for her. She learned to fly by jumping off small cliffs and running through flat fields. She learned to breathe ice and snow through controlling her emotions and finding a place of mental clarity, which she taught herself. Stella and Fin were both misunderstood in their communities. They were both destined to learn their own lessons.

Fin developed his own technique to communicate with Stella. It took much less effort than everyone else's techniques. He would sit with his legs crossed in front of her. He would slow his breathing as his mother had taught him. Fin would then relax every muscle in his body.

He would become aware of his toes; then, he would relax them. He would place his mind on noticing his feet and then relax them. Then his legs, torso, arms, etc., Fin would feel as though his body were melting into the earth. That is when the lines of communication would open wide up. He could almost hear his dragon's words; every thought was coming in so clearly.

The more that the two got to know one another, the more they learned from each other. Fin realized that as long as he was in Maritown, he would never appreciate the life that he had been given. He and Stella came up with a plan that involved the two of them traveling around the world. They would find new places and new things to experience.

He told his father and mother that he was going to have to leave town for a year or so in order to find his passion and to learn the lessons that he was incapable of learning inside the city walls. They were both very hesitant to let their son go, but they trusted his companion. This was also the first time that either of them had ever seen him so interested in something. Fin's parents were so proud that he was growing into a strong and intelligent man.

His parents also came to the realization that they had been wrong about their son. That what had looked like apathy, was really an inability to learn in the same way that others do. He was a smart young man, but he was going to have to take his own path. All he had ever known was luxury, and he could never develop while he was given everything with little to no effort. He wanted to be worthy of a family of his own one day. He wanted to have children. Most importantly, he was going to come home to Maritown and that is all that his mom and dad could ever want. They wished him luck and told the young man that they loved him. They smiled as he rode atop of Stella's back as she flew into the sunset. Both Fin and his family could not wait to see who he would become.

Chapter 5: A Standout Tail

Meditation and taking care of mental health has always been very important to the dragon community. Destressing is an important part of being able to access hidden powers. The dragons can feel as though they are under a lot of pressure to be perfect, which can be stressful.

There was once a young dragon named Ben who struggled with this very issue. No matter how much be tried on his own, he was unable to relax for very long. This began to cause issues with his powers because he was unable to control them.

Ben was also a very special dragon, but he was unable to see his worth. He doubted his own worth because his powers were so far beyond his ability to control. He was a young dragon with copper scales. He was able to manifest metal in weirdly shaped globs, sometimes. This was a strange ability to have, by all accounts. It was very out of the ordinary for a creature to be able to create things out of thin air. Mainly, dragons were able to control the elements. They were not magic in the way that they could just zap a thing into existence.

This young dragon was also very sensitive, which can sometimes spell trouble for the ability to manage powers. It can be so trying for a dragon to have to overlook their basest impulses, but powerful emotions have the tendency to cause havoc in the dragon community. Nothing is more frustrating than accidentally allowing yourself to coat everything around you in a thin dusting of silver.

Ben was a kind and empathetic soul, which also made things difficult for him. Whenever he was scolded, he took it personally, and the situation usually ended with the poor dragon having to isolate himself so that he didn't just materialize steel mounds. Sometimes, it could be easier just to stay away from everyone else to keep from messing things up.

He tried to hard to be calm and likable, but he just could not help but lose control. His emotions were too powerful. He began to spend most of his time away from everyone else in his community. His family was sad to see him in this state, but they also wanted to do everything within their power to keep everyone else safe from his spells of malcontent.

Ben would patrol the woods for hours. He wasn't one of those dragons who enjoyed the time to themselves. He longed to have someone to talk to, someone to understand him. Sometimes he would even make up other dragons in his head so that he had someone to talk to. This allowed him to socialize with dragons that would not judge him for his shortcomings.

One day, the community was having a celebration of the solstice. This family and all of his peers would be attending. His mother had asked the young dragon, apprehensively, if he would be going to. Ben caught her hint and told her that he would not be able to make it. It hurt him to see her breathe a sigh of relief to the news that he would not be causing any issues during the party.

As the rest of the dragons gathered to begin their feast, Ben snuck off to the woods to watch from a distance. Gold dust was following him as he walked because he was so saddened by the fact that he was always going to be excluded. He had tried all of their advice to clear his mind by sitting quietly; that's almost all he did. He decided that he was just going to face it; he was never going to accept.

It was then that he heard a noise in the trees behind him. It looked up to see a small lime toned dragon gazing at him from the branches of a tree. He had no idea how long the smaller dragon had been watching him. Ben could tell that she was going to talk to him; he wasn't sure how to avoid that. He didn't want to; he was so lonely.

The little dragon introduced herself as Hazel. She and her family lived off by themselves at the other end of the forest. She said that she noticed that Ben looked sad and she was curious, so she began watching him from the trees. She was so small; the size of a human child. He was unsure of telling her too much information about himself, but he couldn't help it. The words came tumbling from his mouth.

"I am Ben. I am hiding in the woods because the other dragons don't like me. I tend to make a mess of things when I become emotional. I have destroyed a lot. I can't control my abilities," He said, looking down.

"Have you hurt anyone?"

"Well, no, but I have ruined a lot of grass..." Ben said. Hazel began to laugh.

"We have so much grass... I just don't understand why that matters, I guess." Hazel said.

"It does though. No one wants to deal with me. It had made life very hard and lonely for me."

"Do you need a friend?" Hazel asked.

"Just like that? You don't know anything about me?" Ben said.

"I know that you hang out in the woods because you don't want to damage grass, and I think that is hilarious, so I am pretty sure that we could be friends," Hazel said, laughing again.

"It isn't just me! It's everyone I live around. They all avoid me. I can materialize metal out of thin air. Everyone is afraid of me."

"WHAT?! That is incredible. I have never seen that ability before."
Hazel said.

"I can't control it, that's the thing..."

"We are made to control our powers. You can control it; you just have to learn how. You aren't a lost cause or anything. In fact, that is the most impressive and useful gift I have ever heard of." Hazel said.
Ben's eyes grew wide. He could not believe what he was hearing. He had tried for so long to get a handle on his gift. What if he had been looking at this wrong the whole time. Ben was also out of ideas as to how to master his abilities; he had tried everything that had worked for the other dragons. Maybe it's just that he was not like the other dragons.

Ben and Hazel became fast friends. They made time to see one another every day. Hazel decided that she was going to be the one to help Ben get a grasp on his metal producing powers. The two worked tirelessly toward their goal. Ben was, unfortunately, a tough egg to crack, but he was great company.

Hazel had grown up in the forest. Her family was a rare breed of tree dragon, and they were much smaller than others. For this reason, her family chose to keep to themselves in the trees. Hazel had a secret pertaining to her family that she had been keeping from Ben; she knew that she would have to tell him sooner or later.

One particular evening, Ben was very distraught. His family was questioning him about making progress toward being in control of his abilities, and he had to tell them that nothing had changed. They knew that he had been going to the woods every day in an effort to master his powers. He felt terrible, which made it difficult to not cause a spewing of metal. He ran to the woods with tears rolling down his cheeks.

When Hazel saw her friend, she told him that she needed to tell him something. Her father is a dragon tutor. He works with other dragons to help them find their control. She wanted to be the one to help her only friend, so she hadn't told him, but she felt like it was time to introduce the two of them. Her father would be much more qualified to help the young dragon. Ben forgave Hazel instantly and was happy to have such a devoted and kind friend in his life.

Her father was also very small. Her whole family was tiny compared to normal dragons. Ben didn't mind this, because it made her even more special to him. Hazel's dad was so welcoming to the young man. He could read him instantly and knew that he was having issues with control. The two of them make plans to meet up every day until Ben had his metal under control.

Ben went home that night feeling happy for the first time in a long time. He wasn't going to tell his family because he wanted it to be a surprise. The young dragon did not want to let them down again. It was going to take a lot of work to get his abilities under his own direction. He was willing to do whatever it took to make things work for him.

During their first lesson, Hazel's father explained the importance of daily meditation. Especially for a dragon that was so emotional. Being emotional is wonderful and beautiful, but it can also make you impulsive. Ben's low impulse control was causing a lot of issues in his life, and he was ready to change that.

Hazel was present at every lesson to offer emotional encouragement. There was a lot of work that had to be done, but Hazel's father was an excellent teacher. He was learning more than he ever had from taking the lessons in his community.

After months and months of worth, the team finally found the right meditation for Ben. They unleashed his full potential through a guided meditation that he could take with him anywhere. Ben was so successful for the first time after the following visualization:

Take a seat somewhere upright. You do not have to cross your legs for this. You could also be lying down. Breath slowly to counts of four, in through your nose and out through your mouth. Picture a glowing ball of healing light in the sky. Ben's ball was blue because that was his favorite color. Your orb may also be colored accordingly. Watch it as it travels from the heavens, slowly down to you. It is getting closer and closer.

Allow the orb to land in front of you and watch as it consumes your feet. There is warmth and healing energy radiating away from the orb, and you can feel it in your toes and then the soles of your feet. It is vibrating and glowing.

As the orb begins to grow, it consumes you more. Your legs are now inside the healing orb. You feel its warmth covers your legs. Feel it drawing the tension from your muscles. Feel its heat relaxing every part of you that it touches.

Watch the orb as it continues to climb over you, releasing the rest of your bodily tension. Take deep breaths and bring the light inside of you. Allow the healing power into your body.

Sit and enjoy your orb for as long as you need to. This exercise can be done anywhere and should leave you feeling like you have just enjoyed a day at the spa. Ben was able to finally gain control of his emotion through this meditation.

For the first time in his life, he was intentionally creating metal. The more that he and hazel's father worked with his abilities, the more he was able to manipulate his gift. Only weeks had passed when Ben first materialized a rock. He was growing more and more competent with his gifts. This allowed him to accomplish incredible feats.

The young dragon kept this discovery a secret from his family because he wanted to see how far he could take his power. He was finally feeling self-confident about the dragon that he had become, and he was excited about the future. He was going home every single day with a smile on his face.

One day he and Hazel were practicing in the forest when he tried something new, and it worked. Both dragons stood there, amazed at the small metal and rock structure that stood before them. He had created a shelter. He was able to dream buildings into existence. What followed this was a wave of new experiments. He made a treehouse for Hazel's family. He was creating the most astounding works of art, including metal and stone replicas of his new friend and her family. All of his newfound gifts were breath-taking, but he had no idea of the scale of their usefulness until one fateful day.

He was at home in his family's cave one day when he heard the news that they were being required to evacuate. The young dragon and his family all fled from their cave just in time. There was a landslide that took out the entire community's cave system. No one was hurt, but everyone was devastated. They were going to have to find a new place to live. Everything about their lives was going to change. Ben realized that moving might mean less contact with his best friend, who lived in the woods just beyond their mountain field.

Without uttering a word, Ben centered himself and began to work. He materialized an entirely new cave system. It was a massive undertaking, and he could feel his powers draining as it was happening, but before their very eyes, a new home arose from the rubble.

The community was dumbfounded. Their homes were all much larger, and there were corridors and communal rooms. No one was limited to tight quarters any longer and he had completely cleared the rubble. Ben was praised as a hero. His family was awestruck by Ben's work.

He had to rest immediately following this, but the community got together and discussed his achievement. He was given his own holiday that was celebrated on that same day every year. His parents were so proud of their son. He had finally gained the respect that he had always dreamed of and was able to maintain his friendship with Hazel. Ben had learned the long and hard way, that he was special. He should never have held his achievements up against those of his peers because he was destined to take a different path.

Chapter 6: Mending the Fissure

Blu was a young dragon living in the remote rainforest region of Ker in Obligant. Ker was a dragon paradise. The community that lived there had absolutely no interaction with humans and no expectations. Life was about only what the dragons wanted it to be about. This was an ancient and mountainous land that was occupied only by creatures who could survive the exotic insects and near-constant rainfall. In some areas, the light didn't even penetrate to the forest floor; the animals lived in perpetual night. Blu loved the darkness, but he traveled all around the region, his community was always on the move.

He was named for his color. It isn't the sharp blue that you are imagining. The young dragon is the shade of midnight. He is the bluish-black of a raven's feathers. His eyes are deep violet. His darkness was rumored to come from his birth during the sapphire moon.

Blu had always been a confident outsider. He loved his community, but they did not always understand him. He spent a lot of time alone. He had a difficult time relating to the small group of dragons that he knew. They were all so concerned with sharpening their powers, but for what? There had to be more to existence than being stronger than everyone else.

Life was miraculous in the rainforest. So many creatures of so many different creatures of varying size and color. Blu would spend his days relaxing on a branch as the tropical birds carried magical tunes. His absolute most favorite part of living in a tropical utopia? The fruit. The honey-sweet and sinfully delicious tree fruit was Blu's favorite. He loved the taste so much that he made fruit tasting into a hobby.

The curious dragon would roam the forest and for hundreds of miles in every direction in search of exotic fruit. He wanted to see and taste everything. He had even become quite knowledgeable about pairing tastes together, something that dragons are not known to be good at. He was magic's answer to a chef. Blu preferred these adventures to the company of his peers.

One warm day, he was roaming over a mountain that he had never visited before. The sun was shooting through the canopy like spotlights, and the young dragon made a game out of never touching the beams. Chipper birds chirped away their cares as the dragon passed through. Blu was his happiest when roaming through nature alone. There was something so satisfying discovering a new place, somewhere that he hadn't been before.

Just ahead of him was a threshold that seemed to be made of two trees entwined together at the top. It looked magic and intentional. The young dragon thought that maybe this was a sign that he should turn back instead of progressing forward, but something inside him told him to keep pressing on. The whole area seemed to be glowing in a way that didn't make sense to Blu. He wasn't one to shy away from adventure, though, so he cautiously began to sniff around the trees.

He thought that he could perhaps be entering an area that was once occupied by humans or something else. There were a lot of ruins in the old forest. Buildings that sat quietly as the hands of time turned the years away. He suspected that maybe the tree gateway that a marker that he was about to come across one such area.

Blu took his time to ensure that there were no surprises. He didn't want some unknown creature to jump out at him. The leaves of the trees were dripping with condensation, causing the area to look downright peaceful. This was his favorite time of day to roam around.

Blu walked through the connected trees, seeing nothing in the way of other life. There were some very interesting trees within the confines. He had seen most of the different vegetation within the woods, but he was witnessing something completely new. The young dragon's heart filled with joy at the thought of discovery. He bounced about like a child, eager to enjoy his spoils.

The further he progressed along his path, the more his surroundings seemed to change. The path that he was walking was slowly becoming more defined, and he could not help but feel that he was going somewhere. Everything around him seemed to be placed there intentionally. Trees lines he dirt path and were becoming less random and more evenly spaced. He was still looking for fruit, which he had seen none of yet.

Which is attention placed neatly on the new flora, he missed the movement that was occurring his side: a clearing on the path that he had yet to notice. A unicorn was taking its midday nap among the trees and flowers. Its iridescent horn looked like a jewel on the forest floor. The unicorn was a stormy grey color with a long pale mane that flowed about his neck.

Unicorns and dragons did not get along. There was a time many years ago when the two species were as entwined as humans and dragons are now. Jealousy and competition had driven the two creatures apart. Unicorns often kept to their own land in the same areas in which the dragons dwelled. They, unfortunately, enjoyed the same spaces, so they tried to keep their distance from one another.

The unicorn rose his head up, startled by the young dragon that it had noticed before. He had never seen a dragon in person before and was taken aback by the creature's features. It took Blu a while to notice that he was being watched from the brush.

The unicorn was not looking on in malice, but rather fascination.

Blu gasped when he noticed the unicorn. He was immediately interested, as he had also never seen a unicorn before. He realized that be must have wandered into their area by mistake. The young dragon was also very nervous about being in the presence of a creature that was meant to dislike him based on his species. He knew that the unicorn might think that he meant harm by accidentally venturing into their side of the forest. The two creatures could communicate through a mental dialogue with one another.

"H-hello... I don't mean any harm. I didn't realize...." Said Blu

"You must be lost." Said the unicorn, with a laugh.

"I like to wander around. I thought that this might be ancient ruins, and I wanted to explore. I am so sorry. I will leave at once." Blu replied.

"These aren't ruins, but I know where some pretty cool ruins are. You want to go and check them out?" The unicorn said. His community would be furious that he was offering to entertain a dragon, but he was so fascinated by the creature that he wanted to know more.

"Yes! That sounds wonderful. Won't you get in trouble?" Blu said.

"I could, I guess. But so could you. Maybe we could just go explore for a few minutes, and no one has to know.

"Okay perfect! Lead the way." Blu said.

As the two walked back out of the unicorn's domain, they began to get to know one another. The unicorn's name was Poe, and he was a lot like Blu. They were both lonely adventurers who enjoyed the thrill involved in finding new places. Blu told the unicorn all about his fruit fascination, which intrigued his counterpart. He told the dragon that he could see himself having a lot of fun going on the hunt for new fruits.

Both of them had longed for a friend who shared their interests, and both of them had never found that friend within their own camps. As they trekked along a winding path, the two of them could not help but feel hopeful about their future. They were so invested in the conversation and the company that the other offered. Neither of them said a word about the ancient grudge between their species because they wished to live in the moment just a bit longer.

Poe led Blu to a clearing that seemed to go on forever. There was a wide strip of land where trees were not growing; instead, it was covered with tall grass. The young dragon had never witnessed anything like it and was eager to get to know this new place.

Direct sunlight was also something that Blu had never been accustomed to. Poe laughed as the dragon seemed to squint at the exposure. The pair also shared the same sense of humor. Blu and Poe cracked jokes to one another as they walked. The conversation also began to turn deeper as the young dragon vented his frustrations with his community, and then Poe did the same. They were too similar not to be close friends, but both of them understood that keeping their friendship a secret was going to be a challenging task.

The ruins were magnificent and well preserved. Clay buildings stood tall against the jungle backdrop, illuminated in the golden light of the sun. The clearing looked to have been made specifically for this ancient village. There were large buildings were the citizens probably went to church. There residential structures.

The inside of these clay monuments was painted with brilliant, bold colors. They displayed various magical creatures interacting with the villagers. These murals included plenty of dragons and unicorns, and the pair had the same thought at the same time. What if they were looking at images of their great great great great grandparents? What if these creatures were their ancestors and this was a testament to the harmony that was possible between the species. The new friends were very solemn and thoughtful at the sight of these images. Poe had never looked at the murals up close like that before.

Without saying a word, they decided that they were going to carry on with a secret friendship. They were going to meet up and have meaningful conversations. They were going to spend time together. The petty and unwarranted judgments of their species didn't matter at all to them anymore.

Over the following months, Blu would sneak out to visit Poe, all the time. The two would go exploring together, often finding new places that they both loved. They were interested in the same things; they just happened to appear to be different. This didn't matter very much to either of them.

Poe had this unique ability to communicate via thought to Blu, no matter how far away he was. At night, when they would both go home to their families, they would spend their cracking jokes and talking late into the night. This was just a normal day for the two of them. As time passed, they began to tell each other everything. There were no secrets between them.

Blu taught Poe how to meditate using the Dragon's method. They would practice visualization techniques together. Poe had no idea what would happen if he were to meditate, but Blu suspected that he might find a power that he didn't know he had. That is how all dragons were taught to find their powers when they were still learning the ropes. Blu explained his favorite meditation to Poe:

Take a series of deep breaths in and out. Holding your breath to counts of four. Imagine that you are slowly floating through space. The stars are made up of warm, healing light. As you bump into them, they relieve your muscle's tension, and you feel lighter.

You can spin and drift in any direction. Imagine yourself floating for as long as you like. Feel your muscles unwind in the weightlessness. Feel the energy of space flowing freely through you.

As the two practiced, they realized that Poe could grow things. He was able to grow flowers at first, and then trees. The more they worked, the more intense it got. He grew several fruit trees for his friend. They were filled with the most colorful and sweet fruit that Blu had ever tasted.

After his discovery, Poe decided to tell his mother. He thought that the unicorn community could benefit from the knowledge that meditation opened their minds up to the possibility of having and controlling powers. He showed her how he was able to grow things.

At first, everything went as planned. Then, she began asking about how he discovered this. She kept pushing and pushing for details when he finally snapped. He had wanted to tell her about his best friend for the longest time. She finally pressured him into making the decision.

She was furious. His mother could not believe that he had been going around behind the family's back. He told her that it was because of that silly interspecies grudge, which she then defended. He was beginning to think that he had made a mistake by telling her about his friend when she finally softened up. She told him that she would like to meet Blu, and he agreed.

That night he communicated to his dragon friend that he had told his mother about their friendship. Blu promised that he would do the same. He told his own mother, and her reaction was very similar. They decided that they would each meet the other family and then try to bring the families together.

When Blu arrived at Poe's family's home, there were a lot of eyes fixed upon him. No one in the community was thrilled to have a dragon lurking around their part of the forest. It was a frosty reception, but Blu understood. He was always going to be friends with Poe, anyway. The unicorn community could be as angry about it as they wanted to be.

The meeting was tense at first. The family was not welcoming to Blu. Poe's mother was especially silent. She was very closed-off to the idea of being friends with dragons. Blu told them the story of their meeting. He told them about wandering past the threshold and not knowing where he was. Poe's father seemed to be the most interested in the young dragon.

He asked about Blu's age, and when he was told that the dragon was the same age as his unicorn son, he was immediately more amiable. He was almost downright interested in Blu. He began asking all sorts of questions about his daily life and his family dynamic. Finally, they all began to discuss his friendship with Poe. The father told him that he was glad that his son had a best friend. He always thought that the grudge was silly. These words seemed to also unfreeze Poe's mother. The rest of the evening was spent exchanging stories and having fun.

The meeting with Blu's family went down in a similar fashion. Everyone was hesitant to trust the unicorn until his mother just gave up on the hard act. She was the first of the dragon family to welcome the young unicorn and take a genuine interest in the things that he was saying.

Their ways and customs were all different and fascinating to the other family. They made plans to introduce both families to one another. The evening went better than any of them could have expected. There was an instant connection between the adults.

Soon everyone was admitting that they did not really know the nature of the grudge, only that they were supposed to feel a particular way toward the other species. Eventually, the two friends took their families to see the murals on the walls of the jungle ruins. They all stood before those walls and contemplated everything that they had ever been told.

The rest of their communities have not come around yet, but familiarizing the two families was the first step. Soon everyone else's curiosity will build enough to allow them to begin asking questions. Then they will discover that they have so much in common. Then comes the realization that no one remembers why there was a rift in the first place. Some minds are born open, and others must be opened little by little.

Chapter 7: Price of a Heart

There was a peasant boy named Charlie who lived beneath a castle in a village (called Creston) that was quite poor. The townspeople worked to make money for themselves, but their wages did not afford much. The king taxed his citizens, taking away even more of their income. One would think that with all of this poverty and lack of material possessions, the town's people would be angry or rioting. Quite the opposite.

The people of Creston were some of the happiest in all of Obligant. Other than taxation, they were mostly left alone to live life as they saw fit. The protection of the castle and the king's army meant that they lived their lives in peace. The entire community seemed to operate on a higher level of empathy and compassion. They were Obligant's proof that human nature was inherently good.

Gardening was a favorite pastime for the people of Creston, which made the poor town beautiful. Their rustic wooden cabins peppered the countryside, appearing to be placed down in beds of vibrant flowers. Large trees were planted and nurtured, providing shade in the summer and plenty of fresh air. There were wild creeks and rivers cutting through the land, allowing for lots of swimming and fishing.

The residents of Creston would not have given up their village to live in even the most luxurious of cities. They had everything that they could ever need, right at their fingertips. There was magic in the forests that ran parallel to their lands; so, dragons were integrated into their daily life. The entire town was built upon the principals of love and unity.

They were known for taking in anyone. Should someone appear in the village who needed a place to stay, they were given a warm (albeit small) bed and a meal. This was the case for Charlie, who had no memory of how he ended up in the town. He and his dragon were taken in by a local couple who had decided to raise the boy as their own.

Charlie loved this family, and they loved him. Once he and his dragon had a bath and a few meals, they were both very handsome. Charlie's dragon was named Hem. Hem and Charlie had found one another while the young boy was wandering aimlessly through the woods. If it weren't for Hem, Charlie would probably have been lost forever.

Hem was unlike anything that the town's people had ever seen before. His skin was slick and lacked scales, but it shone with an iridescence that was unheard of. The dragon was possessed of brilliant gold eyes that were flecked with bits of copper and silver. He looked like an opal jewel and captivated all those who met his gaze.

Charlie told his new parents that Hem found him passed out on the forest floor. The dragon had taken the poor child back to his cave to keep him warm and save his life. No one had ever seen a creature like him before because he came from deep in the earth. He was born into a cave that was known for its crystals. No one knew what Hem's power was except for Charlie. He had always told anyone who asked that the dragon would reveal himself when he felt comfortable enough to do so.

The boy and his dragon were inseparable and very protective of one another. That is how the pair had to carry on before the village, and no, it was just habit. Charlie was very careful about the people that he allowed around Hem. His family and close friends were allowed access to his dragon, but he was cautious of others and their intentions.

The townspeople knew of the dragon, but they also cared enough about Charlie not to violate his wishes. Charlie was a nervous boy after everything that he had been through. He was unaware of most of his ordeal before being found by Hem on the ground that day. There was an unbreakable bond between Charlie and his companion. His adopted family was also very close to the boy, and they cared for him as if he was one of their own. Charlie loved his mother and father and would not trade them for anything.

One day Charlie was invited on a camping trip with his father in the forest. The boy decided that Hem should stay behind to ensure that his mother was looked after and protected in their absence. The trip was only supposed to be for one day and one night.

Charlie and his father packed their bags to get ready for the bonding trip. They were going to go into the forest and practice some new meditations to ensure that Charlie was able to stay on top of his mental health. The pair were going to hike to the top of the nearest mountain ridge and take their time getting in touch with nature.

Charlie's mother kissed him goodbye and wished the pair well on their trip. She assured them that they didn't need to worry about things back home and that she and Hem would have a wonderful time in their absence. Charlie hugged his companion dragon and told him that he would miss him while they were away.

When Charlie and his father left, the house was unusually quiet. Hem paced about in boredom for a while before he decided that he would watch Charlie's mother cook. He had always been interested in food and loved the process of preparation. The dragon was smaller than most and roamed around the house just like any other member of the family.

Charlie's mother told Hem that she would prepare him something special to thank him for his companionship. That is when she heard a knock at the door. She answered it to find several very official and regal looking men. They appeared to be trying to look inside her house.

She asked the men if she could help them, wondering what they could possibly want from her. The men told her that on order of the king, they had come to witness the rare dragon that she was housing. She told them that she did not feel comfortable with their meeting Hem, but they pushed past her.

The men were awestruck by the beauty of the dragon. He was sitting on the floor behind the woman, looking rather concerned. His opalescence was something that none of the court's men had ever seen before in their lives. They understood why the king was potentially interested in acquiring the dragon for himself.

Hem was also made nervous by their approach; he could sense that something was off. Dragons have always had the ability to read the intentions of others, as well as thoughts and emotions. They were creatures that were built for perception, and Hem was no different. He was used to being admired, but his loyalty was and had always been to Charlie.

His community and the dragons that looked like him were rarely seen because they had no desire to be passed around like material possessions. They had learned from the naivety of their ancestors that humans tend to value shiny things. Charlie was his person, and he had no desire to change that. He was unimpressed by the expensive riding coats of the men and their many medals and pendants. Who cares if they are important to the king? The king was none of his concern.

To Hem's dismay, they were making a fuss over the dragon. They wanted him to have an audience with their beloved king. They would pay the family handsomely, they said. The family was not interested in money. Charlie's happiness was his mother's priority. There was a growing tension in the room as it became clear that the men meant to take the dragon away.

At first, the men were requesting, and then they were demanding. Hem knew that he would have to go in order to protect the family that he had come to love so much. He was going to have to give in. He wished that he could have anticipated this so that he would have been more prepared. Charlie wasn't even here, and they would not have the chance to say goodbye.

The men made their threats and left with the disheartened dragon. What purpose could he even serve a king? He was too small to ride atop. He was sure that the king had other dragons for that; he was probably just going to be a pretty thing for the people of the court to gawk at.

The cart that Hem was being transported in jumped up and down upon the bumpy road. He could tell that the horses were having a difficult time navigating through the mud and dirt that covered the town's only path out. He was going to miss that road and the hillside. Mostly, he was going to miss Charlie. He had to come up with a plan to free himself from the grasp of the king and return to his companion.

He could hear the men chatting about a number of different things. They were also going on about how pleased the king was going to be to receive the dragon. They were wondering where he was going to live and if he was going to stay in the castle.

When they arrived at the castle, Hem was blown away by the size of it. It was a large stone structure guarded by a moat and a large stone wall. It was both oppressive and stately. There was very little time for the dragon to take in his surroundings after being unloaded, as he was rushed off to a side entrance. It was explained to him that he would be monitored until he settled in and learned to love his new home. The dragon was never going to love his new home, he thought to himself.

The men stood with the dragon on the inside of the castle in a small room until a girl joined them. She was a small and polite young lady with a warm smile. She made the nervous dragon feel a little more at ease. She was sympathetic to the Hem's feelings of displacement. He could not help but immediately trust her.

"I am the king's companion liaison. My name is Anne. I know that you have had a long and difficult day, so I will show you to your quarters. We have a whole wing dedicated to companions; you have a staff that is directed to get you anything you may need. You can see me if anything is unsatisfactory and I will take care of it. I will also come visit to help you adjust." The girl said smiling.

She led Hem to his room so that he could rest before meeting the king. She tried her best to comfort the dragon, telling him that it wasn't going to be so bad. He missed Charlie. His room was luxurious and even had a bed made just for him with a down mattress and lots of pillows. It wasn't the foot of Charlie's bed, though, and he could never appreciate it in that way.

Later that night, the dragon was taken to his meeting with the king. He attempted to not come off as ungrateful or as though he was plotting his escape (because he was). The king was blown away by the color of Hem's skin and the way that it reflected the light. This was the most beautiful dragon that he had ever seen, and he was proud to have him as a member of his court.

Hem found out the king had a number of creature companions and was almost a collector. He guessed that the king probably had not legitimately bonded with any of these creatures, because he wasn't treating them in the way that he would if they were truly connected. If he were connected to a companion, it would spend all of its time with him and not locked away in a wing with a dozen other creatures. They were all being used as decoration.

Hem began asking around, and he found out that this was indeed the truth. He asked the others why they had never tried to escape, and they had a difficult time answering the question. They all had powers, and most of the dragons were not interested in living in the castle. He was sure that it was because they didn't want to incur the king's wrath. He didn't want that either, but he had to find a way out.

He was doing his best to come up with a plan for their escape. Hem was speaking to the other companions and trying to gauge their willingness to try to run. The dragon did not feel as though he was having much success. Most companions seemed content to just live out their days like this. If the king had an actual companion, he would not keep all of these dragons and unicorns locked up together. He would empathize with them because he would care so much for his own partner.

Hem had to try to find a way to find him his own companion. Maybe a sea dragon? He was sure that lots of dragons would be pleased to be connected to a king. That had to be true, right? Where was he going to find one, and how would he get them to connect?

The sweet young lady that had spoken to him earlier came into the companion wing with food for the dragons and marshmallows for the unicorns. Unicorns love marshmallows; he had never understood why. Unicorns are weird anyway.

All of the companions had their own room, it was either a stable or a wooden room with a basking rock, depending on if you were a dragon or a unicorn. Hem pulled the lady into his room when she had finished handing out the sweets. He knows that she would have to meditate in order to speak to him, but he was really hoping that she would be willing.

She was immediately connected. He showed the lady that he was heartbroken, and he was going to have to leave. She conveyed that she didn't know if that was a great idea. Kings are so wrathful. The dragon knew that she was an associate of his, but he was going to have to take the risk. He had to see Charlie again. There was nothing more important than their bond. He then saw a tear fall from the lady's eye. He knew that he must have accidentally sent the thought about Charlie over to her.

She pulled away and told him that she was sorry that she could not help.

Another dragon approached him when Anne had left the corridor. He told Hem that it wasn't worth it to try. Nothing was going to work. The system was rigged against the companions. They were being held in these luxurious lodgings, but they were also being held there against their will.

Hem just could not accept that. He was never going to give up. He also knew that Charlie would not give up either, which is one of the reasons that he was going to have to keep trying. Charlie could get hurt in the process of trying to save him, and then he will never forgive himself.

Before Hem knew it, it was time for his audience with the king. The king was a short man with curly hair and rosy cheeks. He looked much for jolly than he actually was. The king admired his new dragon for a moment and then dismissed the creature. Anne was in the room too, directly by his side. Hem could see that his thoughts from earlier had shaken her up. She looked so distraught.

That night while he was laying on the boulder in his bedroom, he could swear that he heard Charlie calling out to him in thought. He missed Charlie so much. He had vowed that he would never use his power on anyone. Charlie had heard him make the promise and had supported him for the sentiment. If Hem was unable to find another way out, he was going to use it. He had the ability to control minds. It allowed him to enforce behaviors that he wanted to see. Hem had always felt rather sinister when using it, so he vowed that he would no longer do so. He was coming to the realization that he might have to break his promise.

The next few days passed just like the first. There was no news, and nothing really changed. Hem was about to commit to using his gift when Anne popped her head inside his bedroom door and told Hem that she was going to try to help him. Hem could not believe it. He had finally found an ally. He was beyond happy at that moment.

Anne told Hem that she had a plan of her own, and she was going to do everything she could to get him home. The dragon was overjoyed by the news. He wanted nothing more than to return home to the arms of Charlie and his family. Every day that he spent in the castle was just another wasted.

Anne was nowhere to be seen in the following days. Hem was beginning to lose hope again when she entered, but this time with a guard. She pointed to Hem and told them that he was the dragon. He was immediately fearful. What if she had betrayed him? What if she wasn't helping at all?

The guards told Hem to follow them. They led him all the way through the castle and back out to the carriage that he was transported to the castle with. The dragon was confused, but he had no choice but to go with the flow of the situation. So many people were giving him so many orders, and he was trying to obey all of them. Right before they closed the door to the cart, the king grabbed it and looked inside.

He seemed to be looking sadly at Hem. He wasn't looking at the dragon as if he cared about him in any way. It was more like he was going to be losing one of his most prized possessions. This sadness gave the dragon hope that he would soon be free. The carriage door closed, and they began rolling away.

The cart did not wheel the dragon home, though. Instead, he was taken to a cabin in the mountains. Anne opened the door to the cart that he was being kept in and smiled at him. He did not recognize his surroundings.

"I am the king's sister..." Anne said before he even had the chance to ask. "I told him that I wanted you. You must stay here for the next few days, as he is going to visit to make sure that I wasn't lying about keeping you. Then you may run home to your family. I am so sorry about this ordeal."

She was crying. Hem hugged the lady, so thankful that he had not been left all alone in that place. He had never given up hope, and now he was going to see his Charlie again. Which he did. Charlie hugged his friend and vowed to never ever leave the house without him again. Hem was just thrilled to be back where he belonged. In the arms of his family.

Hem and the family spent a lot of time visiting Anne. Charlie and Anne became quite good friends too. They were both connected through a common love for Hem. It was a messy situation, but it placed a lot of things into perspective and gave Charlie and Hem a new outlook. Charlie had been calling to him all of those nights, a call that had been heard loud and clear by his best friend.

Chapter 8: A Bond Beyond Speed

Every year there was a fair held in Dragonbrook, at the heart of Obligant. This city was the companion capital and was more populated than even Maritown. People and their companions flocked from all over the world to participate in the events. For one week, the city turned into a huge festival that was dedicated to the celebration of companions.

There were lots of prizes to be won and fun to be had. People from all overused the vacation as a chance to escape and relax. They were concerned only with further bonding with their companions. These celebrations were also a wonderful chance to network and made for a wonderful chance to meet others who shared similar interests.

There was a huge race at the center of all of the fun. The winning pair of human and companion is given the affection of the entire world and regarded as the champion for the whole year. Winning also has a very nice prize attached to it. There is a special mansion built for the winner every year. This mansion is right near the heart of Dragonbrook, and they are always colossal in size and very elegant. There are enough bedrooms for a small army. These buildings are regarded as priceless, making the race a fierce competition. A mass of prize money was also given to those who made the "top five," with first-place winning a fortune.

To a few of the competitors, this was not a time to relax. It was an event that they had spent all year preparing for. To some, it was the equivalent of the Obligant Olympics. This was the chance for dragons and humans alike to shine in front of their peers. This was also a very important tourism event for Dragonbrook, with a team working tirelessly to promote it around the country and ensure that all events went off without a hitch.

There was a young lady named Marigold, who was quite involved in all of the cities events. She and her companion (a dragon named Lilly) made an effort to involved in all community activities that encouraged others to seek out companions of their own. She was a darling of the city, beautiful and kind to a fault. She was willing to go the extra mile with every project she took on. She and her companion had a bond stronger than steel.

Marigold and Lilly would bond every morning and evening. They were so in touch from all their bonding that they were able to share thoughts without constant meditation. Marigold loved this and thought that it was a sign that humans were meant to have companions. Lilly was a gray desert dragon, small for her species with lovely dark and expressive eyes. Others may have thought Lilly to be plain, but to Marigold, she was the most beautiful dragon in the world.

When Marigold woke in the morning, she would face her dragon and begin daily meditations. They would both remain silent, as to begin the process of ridding unnecessary thoughts. The two of them always felt connected, and this was their secret, they were always willing to take the time to bond.

Marigold had to focus on slowing her breathing. She would pretend that there was a bubble in her stomach that she was tasked with inflating. The young lady would take long and deep breaths in through her nose, holding them for around four seconds. She would also exhale slowly from her mouth. She and her dragon companion would sync their breathing to make it easier for the two of them to connect.

The trick to relaxing is to focus on your breathing. This is something that you could do too. Slow and deep breaths. Just listen to the slow and steady sounds of your breath as you find your own rhythm. You can be sitting, or you could even be lying down. It is important that you don't become frustrated by your wandering thoughts. If you catch your mind running away from you, all you have to do is listen again to the sound of your own breath. Wonderful things happen when our minds are clear.

Meditation has the ability to relax and destress us. Sometimes we can be so focused on a problem at hand or a worry, that we let these things set up residence in our minds. You can change this through meditation and clearing your mind. It allows our brain to take out the trash. We can be so close to our own issues that we forget how tiny they are. Relaxing and righting your thoughts can be the first step in changing the way that you react to anger or sadness. It can also be a wonderful tool to achieve a better night's rest. Controlling your breath can change your body's physical response to situations.

You can meditate with breathing exercises, or you can carve out your own way. Did you realize that counting sheep is a form of meditation? Next time you are lying in bed, and you are unable to fall asleep, picture yourself in a field. You are surrounded by fragrant flowers that are all swaying gently in the breeze. Imagine that you can feel that wind softly hitting your body as you sit. Butterflies and dragonflies buzz by you as they dance along their way. You can hear the sound of a babbling brook somewhere near you characterized by the sound of water splashing the river rocks. Stay here and relax for as long as you need to. Bask in the sunlight and listen to the sounds of nature. You can change this field in any way that you like, as long as it is calming for you.

Breath control and meditations like the one above are something that Marigold took a grand interest in. As the spokeswoman for dragon and human companionship, communication with the companion was one of the most important aspects of her studies. She championed new methods to find your center, some of which we will discuss later in the chapter. Marigold was an admirable young lady with a lot of time invested in her cause. She was going to school to be a dragon doctor, a profession that was always in demand.

On the days leading up to the festival and the race, Marigold was insanely busy. She could be seen in close towns, passing out fliers and engaging with residents. Lilly would sometimes fly her further away so that they could ensure the news of the festival has made it all the way inland. There was so much effort put into the organization of these gatherings. There was food to be ordered, tents to be set up, the entire length of the race needed to be indicated with markers, donors, needed to be called up, and so much more. Marigold was thankful that she had a partner like Lilly to help.

The race this year was going to be such a spectacle. There was going to be such a celebration for the winner and the other competitors. Balloons, fireworks, and food would allow the citizens of the community to come together over something positive. Marigold smiled to herself as she thought about how well everything was going to go this year. The trouble with issues is that no one ever anticipates them.

There was a very strong and quick dragon named Cyrus. He was one of a kind, a physical masterpiece. He was muscular, and his features were all so sharp, which made him extremely aerodynamic. Everyone already knew that he was going to win the race with his human companion. So many of the contestants heard that he had entered again, and they immediately dropped out. This was becoming such a problem that they were running out of dragons who would be willing to compete in the race that was at the center of all of the festival activities.

This year's race was a path that was created in secret. Only the designers and the people who marked off the path knew where it was. Marigold had heard so many rumors about it, but she hadn't seen it in person. The team who designed it wanted to make sure that it was more than physical ability put to the test. Being fit and strong was going to be a large part of it, but so was being quick and intelligent. Cyrus and his human companion Mason had scared away almost everyone.

They were down to one other dragon, another very strong contender. Marigold had heard that he was having second thoughts, so she set off to find him so that she might talk him into keeping his place in the race. When he found out that he and his dragon were the only ones left against Cyrus, he was shellshocked and demanded to be pulled out immediately. Marigold told him that he would be guaranteed a huge cash prize even if he lost because that would technically be second place. The man informed her that he was already rich and had no need for the money. For him, this would be more about pride.

Marigold returned home that night, downright distraught. She had no idea what to do about the race. If the entire town had shown up to only see one dragon running the course, then a lot of people would probably be upset, and that just isn't what she wanted.

That night when she was bonding with Lilly, the dragon suggested that she go and campaign in Balmy Valley. Tropical dragons are faster than everyone else by nature. They are much smaller and have the ability to gain so much speed when they are flying that sometimes you wouldn't even see them fly past you. Marigold told her companion that her idea was excellent, and they would set off for the Valley in the morning.

The two of them did their nighttime meditations to ensure that they would achieve a good night's sleep before their trip tomorrow. Both Lilly and Marigold imagined that they were floating in the blackness of space. Just drifting along to the flow of the stars. The stars were all tiny flecks of glitter in the sky. The pale moon was singing a lullaby; her voice was as sweet as nectar. The notes that she hit rang out over the pair, and they smiled at one another as they began to fall asleep.

Their trip to Balmy Valley was a blast. The two got the chance to experience a lot of things that they had never seen before. So many wonderful and exotic trees and plants. There were also so many kinds of dragons. She found one other dragon that was willing to compete in the race; his name was Avery. He was a lovely young moss-colored dragon who seemed to be just coming into his own and learning to be confident. Self-confidence is one of the dragon race's most important credos.

Marigold was so pleased to have enlisted the help of another dragon for the race, but it did not come without a price. To encourage his involvement, Lilly had offered to enter into the competition too. Lilly was so smart and actually quite fast (especially for a desert dragon), but she hadn't been prepared for this at all.

Marigold was so proud of her companion for offering to help another in need, and she had no doubt in her mind that Lilly would do a stellar job. She could do anything that she set her mind to. Lilly, however, was nervous. She knew that she excelled in so many different areas, but she was not convinced that this was one of them. She was concerned that she wouldn't have what it takes to compete.

On the day of the race, Marigold and Lilly did their usual morning meditation. The pair worked on their breathing to control Lilly's fears of doing badly in the race. Their techniques were not working as well as they usually, and it was because that day was such a huge day for them both. Lilly was worried about letting everyone down.

Marigold saw the worry in her friend's eyes and decided that the needed to pull out a special mediation today. One that she had been working on for a while. She was going to lead Lilly through a guided meditation; you can follow along from home.

"Close your eyes and take five deep breaths, in through your nose and out through your mouth. Don't rush them, hold the air in your belly for a count of four and then breathe out slowly. Good, now focus your attention on your toes. Become aware of them, as if you were about to move them, but don't. Then relax them in the same way you would if you do when you untense your face or arms. Become aware of your feet. Now relax them. Become aware of your lower legs...then relax them. Upper legs this time and then relax them. Become aware of your stomach and then relax. Bring awareness to your chest...and then relax it. Arms now, and then relax them. Turn your awareness to your shoulders, and then relax them. Your neck, and then relax it. Become aware of your head and face, and then un-tense and relax it. You should feel like jelly now as if your body is completely limp.

Imagine that you are slowly melting into the bed or floor beneath you. As you listen to your breath, feel your muscles turning into water. Water that is free to go wherever it pleases and can do anything that it wishes. Keep on melting until your whole body is liquid, and you feel completely free. Feel yourself rolling in the way that fluid does.

Now you are being evaporated into the air. Little by little, you are changing form again until you are completely gas. You float up and up and up until you are a cloud. You feel weightless and buoyant, lingering in the sky with the other clouds. You can feel the air cycling through your body as you twist and turn. You slowly begin to regain your weight as you float slowly back down to the ground. As you are turning back into a solid thing from a cloud, I want you to remember the way that it felt to be so high. Remember how it felt to feel like you could do anything because you can and that is still true." Said Marigold as she smiled at her companion.

Lilly was feeling much better, and as though she could at least give the race her best try. She was looking forward to the chance to bond more with Marigold. For the first time in her life, she was going to be a part of the event that she spent all year helping to plan.

They were both excited. They met Avery at the festival; he was looking quite dapper. He had found a person to ride with him, a sweet girl named Ellen. The group of them walked around for a while, taking their time to look at all of the attractions.

Avery told the girls that he had heard Cyrus had not trained at all when he found out that all his most fierce competition had dropped out. He planned to with no preparation. Lilly had not prepared either, but that was not a choice.

"We really need to give him a run for his money, so that he knows we aren't just that easy to beat." Said Marigold.

"I agree...wow!" Said Ellen, pointing to a beautiful pale iridescent dragon accompanied by a young man. There were so many intensely lovely companions here. Marigold spotted a unicorn and a dragon walking side-by-side as if they came to the event together. They were absolutely stunning.

The three teams make their way to the starting line as the horn is about to sound. This noise was an indication that the race was underway. Everyone was nervous at that moment, as the eyes of everyone are upon them. Cyrus has a smug look on his face as if he had already decided that he was going to win.

When the horn sounded, Cyrus barely moved. He began inching forward little by little, mocking his competition. The other two teams took off at lightning speeds. The path was up, over, and through so many obstacles. There were mazes and caves and even a couple of puzzles where the participants had to find clues before they were allowed to advance.

Marigold and Lilly had one giant advantage. Their constant bonding time had given them a mental link, and Lilly knew that Marigold was thinking without having to sit down and meditate. The two of them were zooming through all of the puzzles and making great time. Avery was also doing well. He and Ellen worked very well together.

Marigold and Lilly crossed the finish line first, surprising everyone. They all expected Cyrus to win, including Cyrus. The pair were overjoyed, and Marigold told Lilly that this proves that she can do anything that she wants to do. Cyrus had gotten caught behind in a puzzle. He would have had plenty of time if he hadn't been mocking them in front of everyone,

Avery and Ellen came in a close second. Everyone was overjoyed with the results. The four new friends celebrated the rest of the night by playing games and eating amazing food. Marigold and Lilly decided that they would share their prize with the community and opened the new mansion up t anyone who needed a place to stay. Cyrus learned a hard lesson that he needed to have humility always, and Lilly learned that she should never ever doubt herself again.

Conclusion

Thank you for making it through to the end of *Bedtime Meditation for Kids*. I hope that this book has allowed you to enjoy peaceful nights with your little ones. This book was written with the intention of helping children unwind. It is imperative that children learn the value of self-soothing and relaxation. Bedtime especially can be trying after a long and exciting day. Bedtime stories offer a way to both calm their mind and create memories that will last forever.

Guided meditations that have been disguised as stories provide a valuable way to enable relaxation to children. Stress management can be vital for growing brains. These pages were written to relax and promote a stress-free wind-down before your child falls asleep. The characters in this book empathize key values that parents try to impart to their little ones, including compassion and self-confidence.

This book was written to help children with their fear and self-doubt while also giving them an entertaining narrative. Sleep meditation holds many valuable benefits, and achieving a restful night's sleep can be very difficult when the entire world is still new and exciting to you. I hope that these narratives have allowed you to guide your child to finding slumber naturally. Mental health is one of the most important goals that parents have for their children. Reading relaxing bedtime stories to your kids can be the difference between feeling restful and being restless.

Additionally, if you and your little one enjoyed this book, please take a moment to leave a review on Amazon.

CPSIA information can be obtained
at www.ICGtesting.com
Printed in the USA
BVHW041514220221
600777BV00006B/313